"GET TO IT GET WITH IT GET THROUGH IT"

My Motivational Expression Story

BY: Garrick Wooten

ISBN: 978-1-7357952-2-5

Printed by Power Of Purpose Publishing
www.PopPublishing.com
Atlanta, Ga. 30326

ABOUT THE AUTHOR

Garrick Wooten, a native of West Baltimore, MD. was born June 3rd, 1984. Garrick is the youngest of four siblings from mother Valerie Wooten, (may she rest in peace). He is also an active life member of Omega Psi Phi Fraternity Inc. Garrick was once labeled a menace to society, with no hopes of a future. Mr. Wooten spent most of his juvenile and early adulthood in and out of juvenile facilities, boot camps, adult jails, and prison. Mr. Wooten then received another shot at life with the grace of the Honorable Judge Alfred Nance.

In 2004, Mr. Wooten attended Lincoln University where he became a prominent leader on campus, served on many boards, was a student leader ambassador for incoming freshmen, a resident advisor, and also on the dean's list for four consecutive years. In addition, he was a great role player on the Collegiate men's basketball team. In 2009, Mr. Wooten earned his Bachelor of Science degree in Psychology.

He has over 15 years of experience in the educational field, and has worked with troubled youth in Atlanta, Philadelphia and Ohio. In 2017, Mr. Wooten received his Master's degree in Higher Education. Since then, he's created a nonprofit named 2100 Unlimited Inc.

He also has years of experience working in the entertainment industry working to protect A-list celebrities, and has also appeared on numerous sitcoms. Mr. Wooten prides himself on saving the youth and his slogan is "If you can dream it, it can be done".

DEDICATION

I WANT TO DEDICATE THIS BOOK TO MY BEST FRIEND, JAMES ANDREWS (CHINA WHITE 2100), WHO LOST FIGHT TO CANCER. HE ALWAYS MOTIVATED ME TO CHASE MY DREAMS!

(REST IN HEAVEN BRO)

I ALSO WANT TO DEDICATE THIS BOOK TO MY LITTLE COUSIN, DAVID MCGLAUGHIN, WHOSE LIFE WAS CUT SHORT DUE TO STREET VIOLENCE!

(REST IN HEAVEN LIL COUSIN)

MY MOM, VALARIE WOOTEN, WHO ALWAYS TOLD ME TO BE THE BEST AT EVERYTHING I DO, AND I HAVE A FAVOR ON MY LIFE THAT NO ONE CAN TAKE AWAY!

(REST IN HEAVEN MOM)

"Get to it. Get with it. Get through it."
My Motivational Expression Story

Get to it- Everyone has obstacles they need to hurdle over; the object is to take a moment to identify your problems that you need to work on.

Get with it- Once you identify your problems, you must take on those issues. You must take the time to create and build steps to work on the problems you have identified.

Get through it- You have reached your final steps, which is overcoming the challenges that have been continuously holding you back.

The purpose of this book is to identify your problems, take on your issues, and overcome your obstacles. To help you along your journey, I will be providing prompts and tools throughout to help you navigate through the chapters. While exploring this book, I will share quotes and what it means to me, reflections based on my life's experiences, and provide thought-provoking questions in addition to a poem at the end of each chapter. This will help you Get to it, Get with it, Get through it. Strap on your seatbelt, let's take a ride!

CONTENTS

PART 1

PROLOGUE   2

FACE YOURSELF   4

WALK YOUR OWN JOURNEY   9

I BELIEVE, SO I AM   13

CHANGE IS A MINDSET   17

THE UNIVERSE NEEDS YOU   22

DON'T LET OTHER PEOPLE'S FEAR BECOME YOUR REALITY 25

JUST JUMP   29

WHAT ARE YOU WAITING ON?   32

I PLEDGE TO QUIT   37

TIME IS WORTH MORE THAN MONEY   42

A BLESSING IS A BLESSING   47

BEASTLY HUMBLE   53

GOING THROUGH IT IS LESS RELEVANT THAN GROWING
THROUGH IT   59

MENTORSHIP HELPS BUILD YOUR SUCCESS!   64

AFTERWARD   71

PART 2

LIGHT POEMS   73

DARK POEMS   82

ACKNOWLEDGEMENTS   86

PART 1

PROLOGUE

In life, people tell us that being different is wrong, so, many people never reach their full potential because they lack self-confidence. They lose out on opportunities because they get comfortable with let downs and become accustomed to people telling them no. The vast majority of people where I come from fall victim to the streets or get caught up in the system before the age of 14. I, too, became a statistic of my environment. As much as I had dreams, I was also faced with much adversity, such as peer pressure, drug infestation, broken down homes, etc. With a lack of true mentorship, I started to believe my only option was to survive rather than follow my dreams. I thought that success was overrated.

Today I realize that the Universe had a plan for my life. In the midst of everything I was going through, I was gaining life lessons that helped me be the person I am today. What I learned was some people and situations were placed in parts of my life to help shape my morals, and principles.

I want to thank you, the readers, for believing in me enough to read thus far! Allow me to be your chauffeur to venture into my memoirs. After reading this book, you will never have to count yourself out; you will never feel the need to quit ever again! I will give you quotes that have resonated with me over the years and helped me overcome the adversity and normality of being a statistic in the environment from which I come from. As I drive you down my memory lane, I want you to relax your mind and open your consciousness. Remember, you are in a limo, and each chapter will be partial pit stops into my life that may help shed light on the journey you're on. I am elated to be your chauffeur!

<u>Warning:</u> My life was far from perfect; in fact, it was the complete opposite! All I ask of you, the reader, is to enjoy, learn, open your hearts and prepare your mind to simply understand why I think the way I do, and I will be truthful with all I say. My ultimate goal is to gain alliances that can help save the youth and give hope to people lacking confidence. Are you ready? Let's Go!

FACE YOURSELF

Definition:

Taking responsibility and ownership of one's outcome. Looking in the mirror and really dissecting your life for what it really is, not the way the world sees you.

My reflection:

Reflecting on my life and facing myself, I learned that one of my bad attributes was that I was an attention seeker. I lacked a father figure, so I hated myself and wanted everybody to feel hurt. Before I knew myself, I used to attract all the negative energy. I used to pick fights in schools. I used to agitate my siblings, my friends, and anybody that I was in contact with. It became out of control!

My mom was working at the middle school, and she almost got fired because of my defiance. I was getting whippings in school-- that didn't work. I got kicked out of 4 middle schools-- that didn't work either. I was sent to boarding school-- that didn't work, and I became so problematic that the judge told me I was a menace to society. My mom said she couldn't handle me, so I was shipped off to boot camp for a 90-day sentence that turned into a year and ultimately ended in expulsion. At this point, nothing or no one could face me. I was angry, and I didn't understand why.

I went to my next placement: Victor Cullen Academy for Boys. I had already been locked up for over a year at this point and still hadn't changed. I tried to avoid the fact that I had inner childhood problems. I wasn't trying to face myself, so everyone became a target to feel my wrath.

At the age of 16, the year was 2000, I was sent to Crownsville State hospital for the mentally ill. I hadn't taken anything serious until I was going through intake. I looked in the mirror and said to myself, "I am not 'crazy.' Why am I here?" I found that contrary to beliefs, half of the kids in there weren't "crazy" either. It was a particular situation that made me refocus and completely face myself.

The housing unit I was in was Myer 4, which, I believe, housed boys and girls. My room was right across from the "punishment" room. One day, we were all in the day room, and a girl got into an altercation with the staff, and she spat on the staff. Next thing I heard was "code red Myer 4" repeatedly. The staff then rushed the girl and physically took her back to the "punishment" room. I crept back to my room to see because I just had to see what would happen to me if I acted up. (In regular juvenile facilities, if you become defiant, the staff physically restrain you until you calm down.) What I saw next was completely mind-blowing! You would have thought you were in a scary movie from what I witnessed. The girl was kicking, screaming, spitting, and using curse words. They took her arm, strapped it down, her leg, strapped it down, her other arm, her other leg. It was crazy! Then the icing on the cake: they pulled her pants down mid-level and poked her with a needle. The girl went from cursing and screaming to slow-motion talking, then straight to sleep in a matter of 40 seconds. I was devastated by what I saw.

That was a wake-up call for me. I sat down in my bed and started reflecting on everything that I ever did wrong. I decided that I had to change how I approached things. I went from not participating in groups to being the teacher's pet. I got released from that hospital and sent back to Victor Cullen Academy for Boys and six months later, finally released from there, too. After two years of confinement, I was finally let back into the world.

Moral of the story: If there is an issue everywhere you go then 100 out of 100 times, you are the problem. Face yourself!

Your reflection:

I gathered a few questions from an article I read by (Luenendonk, Martin), titled "15-life-changing-questions-to-ask-your-self-today." These are some self-building questions that can help you live a better life. Answering honestly will have you ready to take on the world. **"I believe in you!"** (note) the article could be found at 15 Life-Changing Questions to Ask Yourself Today)

What is my why?

_____

_____

_____

What am I grateful for?

_____

_____

_____

What are my values, Am I being true to them?

_____

_____

_____

What will be my biggest regret if I die tomorrow?

_____

_____

_____

POEM:

FIGHTING MYSELF

I GOT LOVE IN MY LIFE, PLEASE STAY AWAY FROM MY
SOUL
I'M DRIFTING IN HEAT, BUT MY BODY IS COLD
I CARE FOR LIFE BUT I'M STUCK IN THIS TRAP
THESE HATEFUL SYMBOLS ARE OVERTAKING MY MAP
IS LIFE WORTH LIVING KNOWING WHAT'S HOLDING ME
BACK?
I CAN'T TELL SOMETIME BECAUSE I KEEP FALLING OFF
TRACK
I SMOKE A CIGAR JUST TO SOOTHE MY TROUBLED HEART
I REALLY WISH I TOOK THE BLUE PILL TO REWIND ME BACK
TO THE START BACK TO THE BEGINNING, WHERE THE
TROUBLES WERE NOT SO STRONG I WAS BORN A WINNER
SO I HAVE TO FOLLOW ALONG
THE PATH OF THE CHIEF; WHERE I WAS ALWAYS TAUGHT
TO FIGHT AS I HOP DOWN MEMORY LANE I RECALL MY
MIND BEING BRIGHT I REMEMBER WHEN LIFE HAD ME
CALM AND AT PEACE
I BELIEVE IN HEAVEN SO I WILL NOT RELEASE
THE HANDS OF OUR MAKER BECAUSE THERE IS PEACE IN
THE HANDS I HAD TO GIVE MY LIFE TO THE LORD FOR GOD
KNOWS ALL THE PLANS

WALK YOUR OWN JOURNEY

Definition:

There are times we get caught up comparing our lives to others. We tend to lose sight of what we are called and chosen to do in our life. We must find the path that is set for us to live!

My reflection:

There was a time in my life where I was once lost in the shadows of following other people's footsteps. For example, growing up in the inner city of West Baltimore, I looked up to the guys in the streets, i.e., the drug dealers! I was fascinated with the money, the flashy clothes, the cars, the girls, the jewelry, and I saw the way that people respected them. I looked at myself and the situation I was in (poor, wearing the same clothes, holes in my shoes, going to school with my Sunday best because my mom couldn't afford to have me wearing what was "in.")

I felt cheated at life when I compared my life to the dealers. I saw a value in them instead of believing in myself and following my own path! I said, "Hey, this must be the life for me!" What I didn't realize was my life was simple before I got into the "game!" I failed to see that the poison I was selling to people in my community was tearing down lives. I realized I was being selfish. I didn't care then because I was going to be successful even though what I was doing caused death, both from overdoses and murders. It caused broken homes, leaving children to fend for themselves because their parents were out chasing the drugs I was selling. I didn't realize that close friends become enemies, and that there was hardly any loyalty in the game. However, I knew the rules, so I stuck with my morals, which was loyalty. I didn't know what I signed up for, but I still signed up!

This path that I was on was not my own. I realized that I didn't want my friends to be my enemies; I didn't want kids to feel like I felt with no parents present because they were chasing drugs. I hated myself for what I was doing, but for some reason, I thought I couldn't help myself, and that there were no other options. That's what I thought, and the only road was death or prison! I almost lost my life due to gun violence, and it wasn't until I served time in prison that I realized that the life I was living was not mine. I was the imposter on a journey that was not my own. I accepted my time because it was me that put myself in that situation. However, there was a calling on my life that I couldn't grasp hold of until I went through that phase in my life.

I then took back control of my life and created my true journey! On my journey, I gained knowledge of myself, introspection became a part of my path, and all the things that I was chasing became my own without hurting people. Once I walked my journey, I became the true leader, and 18 years later, I am sharing my story so it can help change your story! TAKE BACK YOUR LIFE! FOLLOW YOUR JOURNEY!"

Your reflection:

Take this time and answer the following questions:

What do you have to gain in choosing your own journey?

_____

_____

_____

What do you value about yourself?

_____

_____

_____

What makes you special?

_____

_____

_____

List five things that you love about yourself.

_____

_____

_____

Answering these questions can help guide you on your own journey to success. Remember you got this!

POEM:

LATE NIGHT EARLY MORNINGS

I GET IT IN ON THE LATE NIGHTS,
AND EARLY IN THE MORNINGS
THE WORDS COME SO VIVID AT THE TIMES OF YOUR
YAWNING
I CAN'T SLEEP, OR REST BECAUSE OF MY RELENTLESS
MESSAGE
THIS IS THE FOOD YOU NEED TO FOLLOW ALONG WITH THIS
PASSAGE
I EARNED MY KEEP I'M SUPPOSE TO BE HERE
GIVING MYSELF TO YOU, THE LISTENERS; NO NEED TO FEAR
THE MORNING, THE PEACE
THE STRETCHING, THE RELEASE
INHALE LOVE, EXHALE THE HATE
KNOCKING DOWN WALLS, REALIZING THE FATE
IMPOSSIBLE IS NOTHING, WHY CARRY THE WEIGHT?
UNDERSTAND WHO YOU ARE, UNDERSTAND YOU ARE
GREAT
UNDERSTAND YOU HAVE KNOWLEDGE, UNDERSTAND YOU
ARE AWAKE
UNDERSTAND YOUR REALNESS, NO NEED FOR THE FAKE
LEAVE WHEN YOU'RE ON TOP, NOT AT YOUR WORST
LEAVE WHEN YOU ARE TOO HIGH TO LET YOUR POTENTIAL
BURST

I BELIEVE, SO I AM

Definition:

Life is about speaking things into existence. Be mindful of what you say because both negative and positive words you utter are true and can become reality.

My reflection:

There were many times in my life where I spoke things into existence, and 90 percent became true. I will share with you three experiences that happened in my life, dating all the way back to the first one I can remember.

I was ten years old in the fifth grade; we had an assignment of what we wanted to be when we grew up, and I yelled out I want to be a celebrity. "Y'all better take my autograph now because I am going to be famous!" All the kids started laughing, but then the girl I had a crush on at the time said, "Let me get your autograph." That's when all the kids lined up and got my autograph.

My confidence was really boosted. This became a self-fulfilling prophecy. Finding myself now, I have been on numerous television shows, released my own songs, performed with, and placed myself around A-List celebrities. Years later, I have become what I believed I could be by putting in the work that was destined for me early on in life.

When I was 13, I ran away from home and was living at a friend's house. One day, we were skipping school and sitting at his dining room table. We were telling each other how we wanted to be big-time drug dealers. We went into vivid details like how many packages a day, all the way up to meetings with other bosses to discuss how we were going to control our blocks. Mind you, I had maybe sold a five-dollar bag of weed up to that point. Within the following six years, I became one of the biggest small-time drug dealers there was. Understand I said small-time, but my name carried weight when it came to some decision making. I had spoken that negativity into my life. With that dream came a lot of hardships and confinement in juvenile facilities, boot camps, foster parent homes, halfway homes, jails, and prison. Please be mindful of the words you use because, at the age of 13, I spoke that negativity into existence. I believed I wanted the drug dealer lifestyle, but now I know that I am greater than that.

I was 19 years of age when I had my third experience, and I remember this day like it was yesterday. I was with my best friend (RIP China-Diggy); the date was around June 24th or 25^{th,} 2003. We were standing on the corner of Vine and Pulaski, and I was out on two bails for felony drug charges. We were talking about how I beat a previous carjacking case out in the County, how God was always on my side, or a horseshoe! The conversation shifted gears to my current situation about me being out on two felony cases. Everyone knows that three strikes in Baltimore automatically equals no bail.

While we were talking, I said, "Bro, what's about to happen is, I'm about to go to jail for about a year and come home and go to college and hoop." He was like, "you're always talking about jail! How the hell are you going to go to college? Nigga you are a drug dealer!" (I'm laughing at this as I am writing because at the time what I was saying sounded really silly.) I was out on two felony bails, the rule is three strikes and you're automatically sitting in jail, with no bail! So I said, "Yo, I just got the feeling I'm going to make out!" He said, "Bro, you crazy!" Then we walked down to Roots and got a drink and some food.

About a week and a half later, I was arrested on July 4th, 2003. I didn't come home until August, Friday the 13th, 2004. That Sunday, the 15th, I was on my way to Lincoln University. I didn't know how because at the time, it was just a wish, a hope, a dream! I believed in myself, and with God's Grace, I gave myself a shot at my dreams. You can, too! Reflecting on my life now, I realize words hold true to what you put in the atmosphere. You will learn in the following chapters how in the midst of that 13 months, I received a ten-year sentence then how I was able to navigate through the system by taking responsibility for my actions. I bet on myself and won!

Your reflection:

I challenge you to dream, why is believing in yourself important?

_____

_____

_____

Now say aloud "I believe that I am great".

I believe I am greater than being normal.

I believe that I love myself! I challenge you to remind yourself every morning to say you are greater than your current situation. So I am! Now write it down 3 times. Congrats you are on your way!

_____

_____

_____

POEM:

A PENNY FOR MY THOUGHTS

I USED TO THINK THAT IT WAS I TO MAKE CERTAIN THINGS HAPPEN IN MY LIFE! BUT THAT WAS DEFERRED REALLY QUICKLY! I USED TO THINK THAT IT WAS ME, MYSELF AND I THAT WAS IN CHARGE OF MY DESTINY BUT THAT TOO WAS DIMINISHED! I FINALLY GAVE MY ENTIRE BLESSING TO THE HEALER AND HE SET ME FREE! NO LONGER AM I STRESSED, NO LONGER AM I THE GUY OF DEFAULT! I AM WHAT HE MADE ME! **A POWERFUL BLACK MAN!** THAT IS POLISHING UP MY SHOES FOR GLORY! I AM A TRUE STORY, NON-FICTION, AND A BLESSING IN DISGUISE! I AM NOT UNDERSTOOD BY MANY, HOWEVER I UNDERSTAND WELL! I HAVE BEEN PUT HERE TO BE A BLESSING TO YOU! I CHALLENGE YOU TO DREAM AND BE WHOLE! THAT'S JUST A MESSAGE TO YOU FROM ME................... WOOTEN

CHANGE IS A MINDSET

Definition:

Results! You can't expect anything different in your life unless you first reform/revamp your mentality.

My reflection:

Many people wonder how I was once a person who had so many felony drug cases against me. Convicted to ten years in prison to turn around and only do 13 months then go straight to college without being on anyone paperwork. Let me tell you. **First of all, I was involved in that life and I got caught! I took full responsibility for my actions!!!** Also, All through the years until I was 19, I never took probation to get released from jail early because I knew what I was going to do when I got home, and I knew the consequences. Even at my young age, I understood that

1. **If I try to take the easy route and take probation, I could end up in a worse situation than I was in.**
2. **If I didn't have an outlet to change, I would be back in jail.**
3. **I knew my worth!**

I wasn't locked up for a violent crime, I graduated from high school, and I had a track record of being a great kid. I was just caught up in my environment. The judge I had that I am forever thankful for is The Honorable Judge Alfred Nance and the ten people that came and spoke on my behalf to help me get another shot at life. None of this would have worked unless I changed my mentality. After receiving the 10-year sentence, I wrote a letter (which is now a poem) to the judge asking for another chance. A few months later, I got back into the courtroom for sentence modification. Ten people spoke on my behalf, and then the Honorable Judge gave me a chance to speak. I took a gamble on my life because I knew the street life was over for me. I told the judge that if he gave me just one chance, he could sentence me to 25 years if I messed up. He then said to me I had to maintain a C+ average in college. I interjected and said, "With all due respect, I will get all A's! Everyone in the courtroom went crazy trying to cut me off, but I was like *no, this is what I'll get*. (**All of this is on public record, by the way**). All and all, the judge gave me another shot!

The moral of this story is I convinced all 10 of my character witnesses as well as the judge to give me another opportunity. But if I hadn't changed my way of thinking, I would have been locked up for 25 years, no college, no career, or anything. You can try to convince and make the whole world believe that you are one way, it may work for a second. However, unless you change your mentality, you will only be a disservice to yourself. Actions speak louder than words!

Your reflection:

This is the time to be completely honest with yourself:

Are you where you want to be in life?

_____

Are you really working hard enough to achieve your goals?

_____

Now is the time to take the mask off and really change your ways. I know you are tired of the same results or going back and forth in the same circle.

Write down your top 3 things that are hindering your success!

1. _____

2. _____

3. _____

Now explain why these 3 negatives once eliminated can help you become successful.

_____

_____

_____

(Note) If I can do it so can you! **"Let's boss up"**!

POEM:

CAN YOU FEEL HIS BREEZE?

TO THE HONORABLE JUDGE THAT HAS HIS LIFE ON HOLD
LISTEN TO THE THINGS THAT TURNED HIS TENDER HEART
COLD
LIFE ON THE STREETS STRUGGLING FOR ENDS TO MEET
GETTING LAUGHED AT IN CLASS SO HE TAKES THE BACK SEAT
HE'S RIDING THE BUS WHEN HIS PEERS ARE RIDING BIG
WHIPS
STUCK IN THE COLD HOMELESS LIFE MAKES YOU FLIP

CAN YOU FEEL HIS BREEZE?

GRADUATED HIGH SCHOOL BUT IT'S KIND OF A CHALLENGE
GUY
HE WANNA ASK FOR HELP BUT THE SYSTEM MADE HIM SHY
SHY TO THE FACT THAT HE KNOWS HE CAN SUCCEED
HE'S STUCK IN THE HOOD THAT MAKES HIM A MIXED BREED
HE'S A TEENAGE KID TRYING TO CHANGE HIS LIFE AROUND
BUT HOW CAN HE BE SUCCESSFUL WHEN HE KEEPS GETTING
TURNED DOWN

CAN YOU FEEL HIS BREEZE?

I UNDERSTAND THE MAIN THING THAT'S HOLDING THE KID
BACK
PEER PRESSURE SUCH AS GIRLS,
WHIPS, MONEY, HOMEBOYS NOW THE KID FELL OFF TRACK
DAMN BUT THE KID GOT SO MUCH POTENTIAL
HE PRAYS TO GOD BUT IT'S NOT THAT SIMPLE
REALTY SETS IN HE'S STUCK IN HIS WAYS
TOO MANY NIGHTS HE SITS AND CRIES FOR BETTER DAYS
AS YOU AND I CAN SEE THE KID IS STARTING TO SLIP

HE'S IN A CONFUSIONAL STATE OF MIND HE GRABS HIS
HEAD AND YELLS SHIIIIIIITTTTTTTT!!!

CAN YOU FEEL HIS BREEZE?

HE'S PACING ADJACENT TO THE MIRROR AS HE SPEAKS TO
HIMSELF
WHY IS THIS KID STRUGGLING ISN'T IT BAD FOR HIS HEALTH?
HE'S IN A POVERTY STAGE ALL HE WANTS TO DO IS PLAY
BALL AND BE FREE
BE A SUCCESSFUL MAN AND GET OUT OF THIS CAPTIVITY

CAN YOU FILL HIS BREEZE?

HE SMILES TO HIMSELF HE'S BACK AT IT AGAIN
NO MORE PEER PRESSURE THAT'S WHAT HE'S TELLING HIS
FRIENDS
BUT THE WHIPS THE DRINKS THE GIRLS HE WANTS IN
OLD FOLKS NOD THEIR HEADS LIKE THERE HE GOES AGAIN
HE'S A CONFUSED YOUNG BROTHER BUT HE REFUSES TO LOSE
HE WANTS TO CHANGE HIS LIFE BUT HE'S STUCK IN OLD
NEWS

CAN YOU FEEL HIS BREEZE?

NOW CAN YOU SEE WHY THIS KID IS TURNING COLD
HE'S STUCK IN THE GHETTO THAT'S A BIG STRONG HOLD
SLEEPLESS NIGHTS IN THE JAIL CELL HURTS
HE STARTS THINKING WHY HE'S PLACED ON THIS EARTH
HE'S ASKING A LOT OF QUESTIONS SO HE CAN BECOME A
BETTER MAN
HE SAID FORGET BEING DOWN; SO HE CREATES A PLAN
HE SAID HE'S NOT DEALING WITH THE CARDS THAT THE
DEALER MAN DELT HIM HE'S GOING TO DEAL HIS OWN
CARDS AND THE DEALER MAN FELT HIM

CAN YOU FEEL HIS BREEZE?

21

THE UNIVERSE NEEDS YOU

Definition:

You are unique! Everyone that is born has a different DNA; no one is born the same. You have to understand that you are great, and once you accept this about yourself, no one can be you more than you. **NOTE!** This chapter is not designed like the other chapters. This chapter is for you to bring light on what makes you stand out from everyone else. **Side bar! Are your seats comfortable in the back? Remember you are in a Limo! Okay! Let's Proceed!**

My reflection:

My energy is above all. When I focus and get into my tunnel vision to accomplish my goals, no one I mean no one- can match my energy! I have the ability to go into any room and change the atmosphere from negative to positive just by my presence. The three qualities that I possess is that no one can compare to me are: I am very intuitive, I am very charismatic, and I am very witty. I have grown to understand myself through experiences, wins and losses, prayer, meditation, and going distances! Sometimes we have to quarantine ourselves away from people, places, and things to truly understand ourselves.

All of these recent tragic atrocities and unfortunate events that have happened so rapidly in a small amount of time of this 2020 year, caused me to value life's meanings, as well as my purpose in life. Quarantining allowed me to hone into my true characteristics that are listed above. These qualities I possess are not for me to gloat; I learned that I was blessed to be a blessing to others. I realized that there are people that really need help, and I would be deemed selfish if I kept what I learned and my gifts all to myself.

Your reflection:

Take a few minutes to figure out what makes you unique. Jot down three qualities that makes you the best version of you

1. _____

2. _____

3. _____

With these three characteristics it's time to put them into action.

Moral of this brief stop is learning who you are can help you build your career and help you to help others. **Remember to have a great day and understand you are unique!**

POEM:

THROUGH THESE WIRES

THROUGH THESE WIRES MY INSPIRATION FLOW,
GUIDED IMPRESSIONS TO LET THE WHOLE WORLD KNOW
THAT MY IV'S PUMPING GOOD OLE POETIC POTION
ENOUGH WORD PLAY, PUN, VERBIAGE SPEAKING IN ONE
MOTION
THESE WIRES ARE FULL OF DEVOTION
A BREATH OF THOUGHT, MIXED WITH AN INTELLECTUAL
EXPLOSION
LIFE IS WHAT YOU MAKE IT! WELL THAT'S WHAT I'M
DEVOTING
A PIECE OF MY LIFE, SPOKEN IN WORDS IS MY PROMOTING
UNDERSTAND I'M VEXED WITH IRRATIONAL IN THE BOX
THINKING
AS MY CONTEXT BUILDS CONFIDENCE, MY UNORTHODOX
WAYS BE SMILING AND WINKING ARE YOU READY?

DON'T LET OTHER PEOPLE'S FEAR BECOME YOUR REALITY

Definition:

Oftentimes people unknowingly and some knowingly project their incompetence and fears onto others. They say things like, "you can't do that!" "Are you sure you want to do that" "that is not a good decision!" "I don't get it!" "That is crazy!" My favorite for me is, "OMG you moving all the way over there?" I hardly ever let people's fears become my reality because I realize I have to be the one to accept the consequences and the wins with the decisions that I make! Sometimes people don't see your vision, and other times people don't want to see your success.

My reflection:

I once was a Dean of Students at Olney Charter school in Philadelphia, with a salary close to 75,000 USD a year plus benefits. To some, that is a great dream job; it was stable, I had my own place, and a car. I loved my job, I loved having an impact on the students, and I enjoyed building and working with the staff and administration at the institution.

At the time of my retirement, I was suffering from depression due to losing my best friend to cancer and my mom with a failed liver in the same year. One night after being up for days, asking myself why this was happening to me, I heard a voice in my head from my best friend saying, "Boy, tighten up! You got this!" and another voice from my mom saying, "Finish your degree, and follow your dreams." That night my mind was made up! No one knew the reason why I made my decision! My friends, associates, coworkers were telling me it wasn't a good choice to leave; I had a lot of people that were doubting me. Some were concerned about my well-being. I respected their feelings; however, I had a vision and dream, so I had to follow my heart and get to my destination.

Fast-forward, I earned my master's degree, I traveled the world protecting and performing, and built great relationships with A-List celebrities. I have been in numerous sitcoms and tv shows as an actor, I have made almost four times my salary as a dean, I have built more relationships, and my journey is not complete yet. None of this would have been possible had I listened to everybody that told me not to do it. I respect all of them for their care and concern, but when you have a vision and a dream, go for it!

Your reflection:

What is it hat you want to do in life?

_____

Now jot down your three top choices.

_____

_____

_____

Now, list two pros and cons of each choice.

1. _____

Pros Cons

_____

_____

2. _____

Pros Cons

_____

_____

3. _____

Pros Cons

_____

_____

When you come up with your decision, research the steps you need to take to follow your dreams. Don't wait! Let's jump-start your greatness right now! Go get a journal, and make google your bestfriend! Well! Besides your chauffeur!! **"Don't deter from your dreams because you can lose out on opportunities through other people's fears!"**

POEM:

MOTIVATION

I WONDER WHAT LIFE HAS IN STORE FOR ME
A TRIBUTE TO THE ONES WHO HAVE BEEN SET FREE
I BELIEVE IN PROGRESSION SO I HAVE TO LEAVE
STEP OUT ON FAITH SO I CAN BE READY FOR WHAT I NEED
TO RECEIVE
I'VE BEEN IN A LOT OF DIFFERENT SITUATIONS THAT CAUSED
ME TO BE THIS WAY SO MOVING FORWARD HELPS ME TO
LEARN HOW TO BE MOTIVATED EVERYDAY A LOT OF PEOPLE
CLAIM THAT LIL OLE ME DOESN'T KNOW HOW TO ACCEPT
HELP BUT I SAY ONE OF THE BIGGEST MOTIVATIONS IS
WHEN I DO IT MYSELF
I LEARNED TO APPRECIATE AND I GRASPED THE TRUE
MEANING OF THE WORD SELF WORTH SO AT THE END OF
THE DAY I FEEL THAT AWE FEELING LIKE THE DAY OF A
CHILD'S BIRTH THE BEST WAY FOR ME TO LEARN IS BY
DOING IT ON MY OWN
BECAUSE AT THE END OF THE DAY I'M THE ONE GOING
THROUGH IT! UNDERSTAND I AM GROWN IT MAKES ME
STRONG TO STEP UP AND OUT WITH NO BOUNDARIES FREE
TO CHOOSE THE RIGHT WAY TO LIVE SO I CAN GATHER UP
MY JEWELS
IM APPRECIATIVE OF YOUR THOUGHTS AND ALL OF WHICH
YOU ADDRESSED
BUT I'M STEPPING OUT AND MOVING FORWARD THIS MOVE
IS FOR THE BEST
IT'S NOT ABOUT THE ROUND OF APPLAUSE OR EVEN THE
STANDING OVATION
IT'S THIS LITTLE DRIVE FROM INSIDE THAT'S GIVING ME MY
MOTIVATION

JUST JUMP

Definition:

In life, sometimes you have to take chances and big risks. Remember the famous quote, "the bigger the risk, the bigger the reward" (author unknown). When one takes a risk, it's a chance to score big or gain some experience. It's simply a win-win!

My reflection:

There was a time I felt I was down on my luck! I had just quit my job working at a club. I was homeless, temporarily staying at a person's house who now I can call my friend, my car got impounded for the second time, I needed to pay for registration and insurance before I could get my car out of the impound. I was scheduled to go to the DMV the next morning with no money, and I hadn't the slightest idea of what to do. I remember this night like it was yesterday. It was around 10:30 at night, maybe at 11 p.m. I got a phone call saying, "Bro, I got a job just for two nights for you. I know it's last minute." I didn't even let him finish the statement. I said, "I will take it." Let me tell you that two nights turned into a tour across the world! I am very thankful for that phone call that night. Needless to say, I never went to get that registration or the car- I left it in the junkyard. When I came back off tour, I bought a new Mercedes Benz C- class.

"Just jump" also means you should always be prepared for any and every time! In the midst of my troubles, I always stay prepared to drop everything and go. A famous quote from the 1995 movie Heat goes, "Don't let yourself get too attached to anything you are not willing to walk out on in 30 seconds flat." I had decided my car became a liability and I was not going to let me not have a car get in the way of a lifetime opportunity! I took the risk and leveled up! You never know what's ahead of you!

Your reflection:

Quick question:

Would you be ready if you were faced with the opportunity to just jump?

With your career path that you chose from the previous chapter, list five tools that can help you be ready when that call comes for you.

List three liabilities that could possibly hinder your progress.

Now turn these liabilities into tools. **I believe in you! You are ready!**

POEM:

A LETTER TO THE WISE

WISDOM OF THE WORLD, THIS IS A LETTER TO THE WISE
I'M SEEING THROUGH A TUNNEL VISION RIGHT WHERE THE
INCEPTION ABIDES THERE IS A TRUTH WE ARE LOOKING FOR;
A PRIZE FOR ALL OF US TO RECEIVE I HOPE WE SHALL FIND
WHAT WE ARE LOOKING FOR, BECAUSE THEN WE WILL
BELIEVE THERE IS A GIFT I BELIEVE THAT THE WORLD MUST
SEE
THIS INSIGHTFUL FRUIT OF LOVE, THAT IS CONTINUOUSLY
BLESSING ME I HAVE GIVEN MY LIFE JUST TO CALL IT MY
HOME
THIS EXPRESSIONIST PIECE BRINGS TOGETHERNESS TO THIS
POEM
I AM A GOD FEARING PERSON WITH A MODERN DAY
APPROACH
I BELIEVE I'VE BEEN SENT HERE TO BE THE PEOPLE'S COACH
I AM HERE TO PREPARE YOUR MINDS FOR WHEN OUR GOD
REIGNS
TRUSTING IN GOD WILL HELP BREAK ALL THE ADVERSITY
AND CHAINS
WHEN YOU CALL ON HIM GREATNESS WILL BE YOUR SHIELD
I AM WRITING TO FORM AN ALLIANCE WITH LIKE MINDS TO
BUILD

WHAT ARE YOU WAITING ON?

Definition:

Procrastinating is the devil! We will lose out on opportunities and blessings by waiting and putting tasks off until later.

My reflection:

One of my hobbies I take pride in is background acting in television shows. If you ask me, I am as important as the leading actors and actresses I work with! The reason why being a background character is equally important is because it brings the overall movie together. Without the background, there are no main characters. It was great and an honor to be working side by side with some great talent. Some of the television shows and sitcoms I have worked on are Walk the Prink (NBA edition), All about the Washington's (club scene), Family Reunion (Charlie Wilson's bodyguard), Growing Up Hip-Hop (Angela Simmons' bodyguard), Love and Hip-hop (Lyrica and A1 Bentley's bodyguard), On My Block (season two Prophet Gang), and In Debt (Club Bouncer).

I got the opportunity for a speaking role after an agency contacted me, but I dropped the ball and missed out on an opportunity to take my acting career to the next level. In this industry, you must jump on an opening when it's first presented to you or you'll lose out! Who knows where my life would have been had I taken that opportunity! The hard lesson I had to learn was life comes at you fast. Never wait until the last minute!

Your reflection:

List a time where you missed out on an opportunity because you put the task off until later. Explain how you could have handled it differently. Last but not least write down 3 ways you can prioritize important tasks. *Hint I gave you one!

_____

_____

_____

POEM:

LIFE'S CHALLENGES

I LOVE FACING LIFE'S CHALLENGES, THE MEANINGFUL
BLESSINGS
ONE LIFE TO LIVE, WITH A GANG OF LESSONS
(I LOVE FACING LIFE'S CHALLENGES, THE MEANINGFUL
BLESSINGS
ONE LIFE TO LIVE, WITH A GANG OF LESSONS)
A CONSTRUCT BULLY FACES TRIALS AND TRIBULATIONS
THE MYSTIC BEING IS IN THE REALEST FORM OF REVELATION
NO TIME FOR DEBATING I'M NOT WAITING
OR IN LAYMAN TERMS NO PROCRASTINATING.
EVERYONE'S WAITING FOR A BLESSING TO COME. WITH NO
SENSE OF MAKING AN EFFORT TO WORK TOWARDS
ESCAPING.
THE MILITARY MIND LEAVES SADNESS IN THE HEARTS
THE MARCH OF LIES NOT ONE HAS BEEN TAUGHT.
I LOVE FACING LIFE'S CHALLENGES, THE MEANINGFUL
BLESSINGS
ONE LIFE TO LIVE, WITH A GANG OF LESSONS
(I LOVE FACING LIFE'S CHALLENGES, THE MEANINGFUL
BLESSINGS
ONE LIFE TO LIVE, WITH A GANG OF LESSONS)
THE CIRCLE AROUND SQUARES ONE WOULD SAY (WHO
CARES)
THE RARE FORM OF BEING
IN WHICH THE NAKED TRUTH U SEEING
A DISTORTED IMAGE OF THE FORSAKEN FRUIT OF
BELIEVING...
AS YOU SIT AND HEAR AT THIS FORMATTED PIECE
AND YOU THINKIN (WHERE)

YOUR MIND IS WONDERING YOU'RE FEELING LIKE YOU
KNOW
BUT YOUR SELF WON'T LET YOU REST (IN HERE)
I LOVE FACING LIFE'S CHALLENGES, THE MEANINGFUL
BLESSINGS
ONE LIFE TO LIVE, WITH A GANG OF LESSONS
(I LOVE FACING LIFE'S CHALLENGES, THE MEANINGFUL
BLESSINGS
ONE LIFE TO LIVE, WITH A GANG OF LESSONS)
CAN YOU VISUALIZE
THE DISGUISE OF LIES
THAT'S PURPOSELY SET IN THE SIMPLEST FORM
THAT HAVE YOU THINKING THIS NIGGA MIND IS GONE
HE IS ALL THE WAY
(OUT THERE)
UNLAWFUL TREATMENT
YOUR WILL POWER HAS BEEN SNATCHED THROUGH BUS
LOADS OF THINKING
YOU ARE BEING DUMBED DOWN BY HYPNOTIZED SINGING.
NO MONEY FOR SCHOOL BUT KEEP YOUR BLING BLINGING.
I LOVE FACING LIFE'S CHALLENGES, THE MEANINGFUL
BLESSINGS
ONE LIFE TO LIVE, WITH A GANG OF LESSONS X2
NOW TURN AND FACE YOURSELF ARE YOU LIKING WHAT U
SEEING
(OVER HERE)
EARTHQUAKES, DISEASE, PLAGUES, MIRROR IMAGES AND
ONE'S LUST
DUMBING THE MINDS DOWN ALL IN THE NAME OF A
DOLLAR YOU TRUST
(UNDER THERE)
IT'S SAD BECAUSE OUT OF ALL THIS WORD TRAFFICKING
TO MOST PEOPLE STILL HAVE THE MAIN QUESTION IN THEIR
HEAD

IS THIS HAPPENING? (WHERE)
I LOVE FACING LIFE'S CHALLENGES, THE MEANINGFUL
BLESSINGS
ONE LIFE TO LIVE, WITH A GANG OF LESSONS X2

I PLEDGE TO QUIT

Definition:

Vices! Anything that has a stronghold on your life. Maturity is a must; anything else you must let go.

My Reflection:

"When I was a child, I spoke as a child. I understood as a child, I thought as a child; but when I became a man, I put away childish things." (1 Corinthians 13:11). I was involved in an accident that altered my life. In turn, it caused me to get a back surgery, and in the midst of my healing I became addicted to opioid painkillers. The thing about the Pks was that it gave me a false sense of feeling. They made me think I was doing better; however, I was not. My addiction grew so strong that the effects pulverized my everyday life.

I could not eat without taking the medicine, I could not sleep, and as far as communicating with people? "Forget about it!" I became a monster! If I didn't have the Pks, I was moody and irritable. I started distancing myself from people that cared about me. I had to quit! Close friends started telling me I wasn't myself! No one knew at the time exactly what my issue was, and I didn't tell them either. I was embarrassed. I was ashamed. I hated myself because I felt like I let so many people down.

My turning point was the day I had a checkup appointment with my doctor. Ironically it fell on 'Yom Kippur (The Day of Atonement, the holiest day of the year for the Jewish faith and is marked each year with a reflection of one's sins, fasting, and prayer). My body was ill! I had aches and pains, I thought it was mainly because of my injuries, but it was mostly because of my addiction. I convinced my doctor to give me more. He gave me a strange look and told me to take it easy! I wasn't myself, and he knew it. I once was high-spirited and patient; always happy. I was beginning to feel fatigued and moody. I was in a dark place! I left the hospital and realized my main pharmacy was closed due to the holiday. My stomach immediately turned, I started sweating profusely, my bones started aching, and the sun just felt like it was doing "waaay too much"! At that moment, I realized it was time for me to stop. I took the pharmacy being closed as a sign from the Most High. To think it was Yom Kippur!

However, I just had to try one last time! There was one more pharmacy in a little plaza next to my doctor's office. I saw that open sign on the door and I knew I had action. I started fixing myself up, ignoring the pain I was going through. I looked in the rear-view mirror to make sure I didn't look like an addict or, in hood terms, a junkie, smoker, fiend, or crackhead. I got out of the car, walked into the pharmacy, and handed the guy the script. Guess what? Denied! I was "screwed!"

I left the pharmacy and threw up immediately. I walked and bought a bottle of water from Subway, got back in the car, and cried. That's when I asked myself, "Really?" "You came this far to disappoint everybody that's in your corner and everybody that looks up to you?" I ripped up the script, and I went cold turkey! Readers, that's the worst way to recover from addiction- I do not recommend it! Seek professional help! However, I wanted to feel every pain, so I could remember how horrible it felt to me; so I would never think about going down that path ever again. It was a tough journey, but I did it! I quit.

Your reflection:

This is a time to be completely honest with yourself.

What are your vices that you know you need to quit?

_____

How do you know that it is affecting your life?

_____

Think of some benefits you will gain once you get rid of that hindrance? *Note it can be anything! Your attitude, anxiety, addiction, people, places, or things. Whatever it is **"you got this! You've already taken the first step by getting this far.**

_____

_____

_____

POEM:

CIRCLES

I'M TRIPPING! ON THIS MYSTERIOUS LINE THAT GOES IN A
TWIST
MY MIND IS FIGHTING AGAINST ITSELF; HIS WEAPON IS A
FIST
THIS FIST IS SO HECTIC IT IS ABOUT TO MAKE ME FLIP
I AM WISHING THIS WAS A MOVIE SO I COULD JUST SKIP
SKIP TO THE GOOD PARTS; WHERE I AM HOLDING UP THE
TORCH
MY GRIND IS GOING NOWHERE I FEEL STALE ON THIS EMPTY
PORCH
HOW CAN I LIVE WITH MASSES OF PAIN?
THEY SAY LIVE MY LIFE BUT IT'S HARD TO COPE IN THE RAIN
I AM A MAN BUT THIS STRESS IS MAKING IT HARD
TO BATTLE WITH SOMETHING THAT KNOWS MY CARD
I LIVE ANYWAY BECAUSE I REFUSE TO LOSE
STUCK WITH THESE MIXED THOUGHTS IS MAKING IT HARD
TO CHOOSE
THE RIGHT YELLOW PATH OR TAKE THIS TREACHEROUS
FLIGHT
I'M BATTLING WITH DEATH AND THEY SEEM TO BE WINNING
THIS FIGHT
I'M SHAPED WITH THE ARMOR AND THE BELT OF GOD
BUT I AM TRAPPED IN THIS CORNER, LOST IN THE FACADE
EMPTINESS IN THE WORLD, BY MYSELF I'M WEAK
IF YOU ARE WHO YOU SAY YOU ARE; HOW AM I SUPPOSED
TO SEEK?
MY SOUL IS HURTING PLEASE HELP ME!
THE ENEMY IS WINNING AND THEY ARE TAKING HOLD OF
THEE
THIS WORLD IS CRAZY AND I FEEL LIKE A LOST PAWN

IN THIS NEW WORLD ORDER, I'VE NEVER BEEN TOO FOND
I SWEAR TO MOSES I AM SCRAMBLING IN THIS PIT
MY STYLE AIN'T CURSING SO I HAVE TO DISPLAY TRUE GRIT!
LEAVE ME ALONE! YOU DESPICABLE LOST IMMORTAL SOUL
I AM GREATER THAN YOU AND I WILL NEVER FOLD
MY LIFE IS IN SHAMBLES BUT I EXPECT TO BE GREAT
MY STYLE IS TO WIN THIS IS NOT UP FOR DEBATE
I AM MORE THAN A CONQUEROR BECAUSE MY GOD SAID SO
SO IF YOU WANT ME THEN YOU WILL HAVE TO STOOP VERY
LOW
BUT LOW IS NOT LOW ENOUGH
AND MY HEART PUMPS PURE BLOOD THAT'S BUILT TO BE
TOUGH

TIME IS WORTH MORE THAN MONEY

Definition:

You can lose money and gain it back with hustle, but you can't ever make up for lost time. Protect your space and your time!

My reflection:

My biggest pet peeve is wasted time. The problem is too many people think that they have forever to be accomplished. So they waste time doing pointless things that can't help them to progress in life. I found that over the years I have grown tired of being in places and talking to people who don't want anything for themselves. I grew to despise giving out advice to people just for them to go and do the same thing over and over and not gain any meaningful results- that is what you call insanity. I call those types of people "energy suckers!"

To associate yourself with me, a person has to want something out of life. People need to have a drive or some type of potential to want to do the right thing. If you are acting and thinking the same way as you were a year ago, I'm not sorry to tell you that your year was wasted. I learned to protect my time. I realized that when I was in a perfectly good mood and talked to someone with poor energy, I suddenly started feeling down in my spirit. Over the years, I had to cut ties with people because every time we conversed, they always complained about how someone did them dirty or "oh, my life ain't right." Then when I offer a solution, they would turn the table on me, like I was the one who made them have that ill feeling! Have you ever had that happen? Your reaction is like, "Wait, what?" I realized that cutting time out to focus on other people's problems that they didn't want to solve gave me more time to focus on myself. In life you are either influencing or being influenced! **Choose wisely!**

Then there are the ones that I call the "outdoers"- they turn everything into a competition. They won't ever let you have a moment! You are like, "I had a bad day," and they turn and say, "Naw, my day was worse." You say, "I got into an accident," and they respond, "Let me tell you about how I got into this car wreck!" You look up and realize you spent half of the day going back and forth with this person talking about absolutely nothing; when you started out just trying to share a little information about your personal real-life situations. Your time should be guarded with your life.

Exclusive! You have to make people understand that your time is worth more than money. I will leave you with a quote: "You'd have to understand how accessible I'm **NOT** to really appreciate how accessible I am to you. Everyone's access isn't granted." (Author unknown.)

Your Reflection:

Take this time to list the five people you associate with the most.

1.

2.

3.

4.

5.

Now, describe the feelings you had after you interacted with these people.

_____

_____

_____

If the majority of your feelings are on the negative side, you must understand you are made up of the 5 people you surround yourself with. The saying is, "If you hang around 5 slackers you will become the 6th one." **If you are a person that falls victim to wasted time, don't worry! Here is your fresh start on a new life. I believe in you.**

POEM:

UNDERSTAND

ALL I ASK OF YOU IS TO **UNDERSTAND**
THE FUNDAMENTAL FACTS THAT MAKE ME A MAN
PLEASE **UNDERSTAND** THAT A GROWN MAN MAKES
MISTAKES
BUT NOT TO THE POINT, IT MAKES YOUR HEART GROW TO
HATE
UNDERSTAND THAT IN TIME ONE HAS TO MOVE ON
HOWEVER, THE LOVE A MAN HAS CAN NEVER BE TORN
UNDERSTAND THAT THINGS MAY SEEM TO GO WRONG
IT'S JUST MISGUIDED IMPRESSIONS THAT ARE HARD TO
FOLLOW ALONG
UNDERSTAND THAT MAN GETS CAUGHT UP IN ILL-GOTTEN
REBUTTALS
THAT CAUSES US TO GET CAUGHT UP IN THEATRICAL
WORLD PUDDLES
UNDERSTAND THAT A MAN SOMETIMES WEARS THE
WORLD'S TROUBLES ON HIS SHOULDERS WHICH CAN LEAD
TO DEPRESSION AND AGGRESSION, THEN CAUSE US MEN TO
BE FALLEN SOLDIERS **UNDERSTAND** WHAT YOU THINK A
MAN IS SUPPOSED TO BE
CAN BE DECEPTIVE BECAUSE ONLY THAT MAN KNOWS
WHAT'S DESTINED FOR HIM TO BE **UNDERSTAND** THAT MAN
HAS ALWAYS GONE THROUGH TRIALS AND TRIBULATIONS
SO WE NEED YOU TO BE A STRONG SUPPORT FACTOR TO
HELP HIS HOPE BE A REVELATION **UNDERSTAND** THAT NO
MAN NEEDS AN EXCUSE
TO BE FALLEN ALONG THE WAYSIDE OF THIS NAKED WORLD
OF ABUSE

UNDERSTAND WE ARE SONS OF KINGS THAT HAVE BEEN
SNATCHED FROM OUR ROOTS TO BE SEEN BY THIS WORLD
THAT TRIES TO MAKE US LESSER THAN WHAT YOU SEE
UNDERSTAND WITHOUT HOPE AND SUPPORT MAN CAN BE
DOOMED
THOUGH THIS STATE OF PURGATORY MINDSET THAT
CAUSES THE WISEST TO BE BUFFOONED **UNDERSTAND** THE
KNOWLEDGE I GIVE YOU TODAY
IS NOT FOR CASUAL READING IT'S FOR YOU TO HELP US TO
PRAY
THAT WE STAY STRONG AND BE WHAT IS MEANT FOR US TO
BE
A MAN
I SAY
A MAN
ALL I ASK OF YOU IS TO **UNDERSTAND**

A BLESSING IS A BLESSING

Definition:

Grateful, appreciation, thankful, and gratitude- these are all words of affirmation to yourself. One must recognize all gifts, big and small. If you are not thankful for the small things, how could you possibly handle and be prepared for the big ones?

My reflections:

I wake up every day, and I thank God because I am provided with the ability to work for whatever I want and need. Waking up gives me a fighting chance to right any wrongs that I may have and gives me a chance to make my good situation great. Who am I not to be grateful for what I have and what I don't have?

There is somebody somewhere praying to God to be in your predicament. I believe being grateful for the simple things in life are a part of all blessings. When you receive a blessing, like freedom, like waking up, somehow finding a meal, an important tool I realized is if we are not careful and appreciate the necessities of life it can be easily stripped away.

Here are two examples of how I fell short of not being grateful for what I had, which cost me to lose everything! One of my first experiences I could remember was when I was around the age of 13. At 13, this is the time when puberty hit, I started feeling myself! I believed that everything my mom was telling me was wrong and everything she was teaching me was basically in the "way" or doing too much. The basic things like take the trash out, or make my bed, hell, get in the shower! Her saying was "You're in my house and you will obey my rules!" Feeling myself so much I rebelled and ran away. Once out in the world I was faced with the harsh reality! "I didn't have a pot to pee in or a window to throw it out of" that's an old saying from the "old folks" meaning the trash that she got on me about, taking out. I became that trash. The bed she told me to make everyday sleeping on steps or hallways was a replacement. Get in the shower she said! Man in those cold streets I was lucky if I could find a sink at a local gas station to take a quick wipe down. The point I'm making is my mom was providing me with all the basic needs that a 13 year old should have and I took it for granted and lost all of it at the time. Guess who went crawling back to my mom begging for forgiveness? You guessed right! Me!

This next experience is for all the people who think taking the route of the street vs working a regular job/ owning your own legit business. I was 17 and a senior in highschool working at UPS. At that time, I was making I believe $10.50 an hour as well as playing basketball for Randallstown High. Side note I was in a foster home in the county because I got labeled a menace to society and got kicked out of Baltimore city public schools because I became too much for my mom to bear! However, a different story for a later time.

So I am a senior in high school, everything is going right. I am earning money to get the necessities I longed for growing up, I am doing my thing in school. The problem came about when I went back to my old neighborhood and I started to compare my life to my peers who were in the streets at the time! Remember in the previous chapter I had just come home from doing a two-year stretch in juvenile detention. You would think that I learned from my mistakes! That little evil thing called **Greed** got the best of me! Jay Z Quote said it the best for me "it's just life, I solemnly swear to change my approach, stop shaving coke, stay away from hoes, put down the toast.

Cause I be doing the most Oh no. But every time I felt that was that, it called me right back. It called me right back, man it called me right back, Oh No!" This perfectly described my dilemma! It didn't happen overnight though. I secretly started calling off of work and sneaking down my old neighborhood as soon as I left school at the times I was supposed to be at work. I started looking at what my peers were making at the time, it tripled what I was making at the job. Let's see! I was making $10.50 an hour working part time. I would bring home roughly $500 every two weeks after taxes. When I would sneak to my old neighborhood I would get a $250 pack of crack which is 25 single baggies of an illegal substance! I would turn in $200 dollars and get $50 dollars give or take off of each pack. 10 packs and I made my salary in a day. This went on for about the remainder of the year, up until I graduated from high school. My foster parents became aware of what I was doing! This became problematic! Everything done in the dark will come out in the light.

Let me explain what I lost because I wanted instant gratification. That $10.50 dollar an hour job was safe, secure, I didn't have any worries. I had ten college offers that were giving scholarships for me to attend school.

UPS was offering a full time position post graduation, also the Independent Living program was setting me up with an apartment where for 6 months they would pay half of the rent and front me 5000 dollars to match whatever money I saved at the job. All of this at the age of 18.

What I gained was a prison cell! The money I was making on the street was not worth what I had lost because when you get locked up you lose everything! I lost my car, I had a 88-Dodge Diplomat, say what you want, that was my baby and I couldn't even drive. I even lost my luxury apartment I had in downtown Baltimore. All the money I had went to lawyer fees and bails. Here is the biggest kicker of them all, In jail, you must work, and guess how much money I was working for? $2.50 a day! Yeah, I said it! **The moral of this story is if you are not grateful for what you have, you will always find yourself in a worse predicament than what you started with.**

Your reflection:

List three things that you are grateful for.

1. _____

2. _____

3. _____

List 3 things that you wish to make better.

1. _____

2. _____

3. _____

Now lift your hands and say,

"I made it to see another day. Thank you for giving me a fighting chance to become a better me." Congratulations! You are now ready for the next level!

POEM:

LIFE

LIVING
IN-STRIVING
FOR
EXTREME
EXCELLENCE
I'M LIVING AND STRIVING FOR EXTREME EXCELLENCE
WHY?
BECAUSE LIFE TO ME IS LIVING IN SUSPENSE
I'M THINKING AND MOVING
I'M LIVING AND GROOVING
I'M FORGIVING AND RULING
I'M PUSHING NOT FOOLING
I'M EXCEEDING AND BELIEVING
I'M FEEDING THE RECEIVING
THESE RHYMES ARE FOR THE SEASON
ASK ME FOR THE REASON
BUNDLES OF JOY
LOVE DOESN'T TOY
I LIVE FOR THE STORY
MY GOD GETS THE GLORY
WALKING IN THE TRUTH
LIFE BREAKS THE ROOF
MY LIFE IS CONTENT
I WILL NOT BE BENT
I'M FOCUSED TO WIN
MY LIFE WITHOUT SIN
I'M DEDICATED TO YOU
WITH MY HEART I'M TRUE
I WILL LIVE MY LIFE
WITH NO PRESSURE AND NO STRIFE

HOW LONG DOES IT TAKE
FOR YOU TO RECEIVE YOUR BREAK
AND
LIVE IN-STRIDE FOR EXTREME EXCELLENCE

BEASTLY HUMBLE

Definition:

One who is self-assured, a team player, a person that will do what it takes to thoroughly complete a task, this person is a doer, not a teller.

My reflection:

I have met some of the most dangerous people a person could ever meet, and I have also met some of the most skilled and talented people that the world has to offer. I learned a key component that they all possess. The majority of them were extremely humble. Someone whose expertise is on high levels doesn't need to be cocky because their skills do the talking for them. In my industry, too much arrogance leads to mistakes, and one mistake can be detrimental to both yourself as well as your clients.

One day I was filling in as an extra bodyguard for a celebrity, one of his guards from the time I met him was boasting about how he was this "ultimate protector." I quickly realized he lacked self-confidence, and I knew I was going to have trouble with him. I remained humble and maintained my professionalism.

As time progressed, he kept trying to get in the way of me effectively doing what I was brought on the job to do. I had reminded him that it's not about either him or me! It's about getting the client home safe and out the way. That talk did not work. It got to the point that when I tried to take position to watch our client, he would rush to beat me to the spot and almost knock the client down. He became so reckless trying to outdo me that he failed to properly store his weapon in a place where it wasn't visible to the public. In turn, the client, myself, and two others were arrested for firearms. I was livid! This was a clear case of incompetency, him not being a team player caused us all to fail as a unit and couldn't complete a simple task that was set for us. This is why I am always humble when I am teamed up with other guards.

If you don't remain cool in situations, you can be faced with what I had to endure, or even worse, you could possibly lose your life. In this bodyguard industry as well as life, one must have codes of ethics to stand on. If not, there is no way a person can be beastly humble.

Your reflection:

1. What does being humble mean to you?

_____

_____

_____

2.Describe what it means to be effective?

_____

_____

_____

3.How can you tie being humble and effective in your life?

_____

_____

_____

Remember, sometimes you have to wait your turn. Never lose your cool in the presence of others. Just simply work harder and create opportunities for your future. Do this quietly, and you will master the keys of being beastly humble.

POEM:

READ OR BE ERASED!

LIFE TO ME IS CHANGING SPACES, BAD TO GOOD MIND
ERASERS.
I LIKE LIVING LIFE, THE BEST; I CAN'T REST BECAUSE IT'S TOO
MUCH ENERGY FIGHTING OFF THE STRESS. I'M LIVING LIFE
TRYING TO FIGHT THE OPPRESSION;
I NEED YOU TO LISTEN SO YOU CAN BE GUIDED INTO THE
NEXT SECTION
WHAT BENEFITS ARE THERE COMING FROM THIS LESSON?
A GANG OF BRILLIANCE, INTUITION, ALL IN THE SAME
SESSION
TOO MUCH UNCLEANLINESS GOING ON, ALL THE RIGHTS
YOU HAVE DONE ARE CHANGING FOR THE WRONG.
YOU FEEL STUCK DOWN RIGHT CRITICAL, AND YOU THINK
YOU CAN'T GO ON. BUT I'M TELLING YOU! YOU CAN AS
LONG AS YOU STAY STRONG.
STAY STRONG! BELIEVE IN SUCCESS; IT'S THE ONLY WAY TO
GO ON.
LIFE TO ME IS A PORTRAIT THAT TOO MANY CAN BE
FOREIGN
HOWEVER I TRY TO LIVE IT WITH THE BEST MENTALITY OF
STAYING STRONG.
YOU MUST GO ON! LIVE LIFE LIKE YOU'RE SUPPOSED TO BE!
A GIFT TO SOMEONE, UNLOCK THE DOORS AND LET YOUR
MIND BE FREE!
JUMBLES OF JOY REALIZING YOU ARE FREE!
UNCHANGEABLE PAST, SO EXPAND TO THE FUTURE
BECAUSE IT'S A LOT TO SEE! BELIEVING IN YOURSELF, YOU
MUST BE ANXIOUS TO BE!
THE NUMBER ONE CANDIDATE THERE COULD POSSIBLY BE.

ENJOYING YOUR LIFE, STUDYING EVERYTHING YOU COULD
POSSIBLY SEE.
EMERGING INTO THIS SUPPLEMENT THAT THE EYES CAN'T
SEE.
TRUSTING IN GOD! SILENCING ALL NEGATIVITY!
ALLOWING YOUR MIND TO BRING OUT ALL THE CREATIVITY!
KNOWLEDGE DON'T YOU SEE!
WISDOM BRINGING A SMILE BECAUSE THIS WAS MADE FOR
YOU TO BE!
WISE YOUNG CHILD! BE ADVISED YOUNG CHILD!
DO OR DIE YOUNG CHILD! OPEN YOUR EYES YOUNG CHILD!
REALIZE YOUNG CHILD! THIS IS YOUR LIFE YOUNG CHILD!
SMILE - YOUNG - CHILD!
BE AWARE OF PEOPLE THAT HAVE AN EVIL TRACE
THE ONES THAT SMILE BUT THE SPITEFUL INTERIOR IS
WRITING ALL OVER THEIR FACE! IT IS A DISGRACE HOW ONE
COULD PLACE
SO MUCH ENERGY IN MAKING THEMSELVES A WASTE!
I TRIED TO DO WRONG BUT IT LEFT A SOUR TASTE.
SO NOW I STAY STRONG SO I WON'T FEEL OUT OF PLACE
A LIFE ALONE HAS ALWAYS BEEN A STRANGE PLACE.
SO LIFT UP YOUR HANDS AND GIVE GOD THE GRACE.
HUMBLE YOURSELF AND GET BACK ON PACE.
RUN TO THE LORD LIKE YOU ARE TRYING TO WIN A RACE!
I'M TRYING TO CONVINCE YOU BECAUSE THIS IS THE TIME
AND THE PLACE.
FOR YOU TO GIVE YOUR LIFE BACK TO HIM BEFORE YOU
LOSE THE RACE.
IT'S NO MORE GAMES TAKE HEED OR BE ERASED!
THE TIME IS HERE PLEASE FALL ON YOUR KNEES AND FACE
THE ONE UP ABOVE WHO HAS THE FLOWERS TO YOUR VASE
THIS IS A LIFE AND DEATH MATTER, WIPE THAT SMILE OFF
YOUR FACE!

THIS IS THE TRUTH!
WAKE UP
OR
BE ERASED

GOING THROUGH IT IS LESS RELEVANT THAN GROWING THROUGH IT

Definition:

Being constantly faced with the same trials and tribulations is like going through a revolving door. You can only get through it when you mature enough to learn from your experiences.

My reflection:

I learned that people grow tired and lose interest in hearing about your problems, especially when you keep doing the same thing over and over. Everyone has limitations when it comes to dealing with people's issues. Let's take me for an example; there were people in my life that are still in my life that love me unconditionally! However, they had to take breaks from me, and I from them because I pushed them to the limit with my issues.

When I was first arrested at 11 years old for stealing a bike, my mother quickly came to my rescue. She believed this had to be a lie because her son would never do such a thing. Second time at 13 for a drug charge, my mom came rushing like the savior she was. By the third and fourth time, arrested for selling drugs, her support started slowing down because she realized she was becoming an enabler of my bad habits. I tried to blame her for not coming to my rescue, but she said I had to learn some things on my own because I just wasn't getting it.

Most people call me lucky because of the experiences I went through in my life. The reason I achieved and overcame many obstacles is because I manned up and grew through the trials and took ownership of my actions. The burden of what I was facing seemed impossible until I kept going. I had to analyze my life. I had to dissect the real issues that kept holding me back. The real issue was I wanted to blame everybody for the crimes I committed, but no one can be my crutch; no one was going to take my hand and walk me through what I needed to learn on my own.

There comes a time in our lives when we have to "GROWTH" up, or you will constantly fail the same test over and over. Let's take school for another example. You are given homework assignments; these assignments are set up to help you prepare for quizzes and tests. You can get over by cheating and having someone do your work, but you are lost and confused when it comes to taking your exam. Just like in life, you cannot cheat it; you have to learn from it and grow.

Your reflection:

1. What does it mean to enable?

_____

_____

_____

2. Give an example of a time where someone came to your rescue when you knew you were clearly wrong.

_____

_____

_____

3. How did you feel?

_____

_____

_____

4. What does maturity mean to you?

_____

_____

_____

5. How can maturity help you in life?

_____

_____

_____

It's time to take back control of your life!

6. Do you feel that you can get far in life if you take responsibility for your actions and not make the same mistakes?

_____

_____

_____

Sure you do! I believe you can do it!

POEM:

GROWING INSTEAD OF GOING

LIVING A LIFE AROUND THE WORLD'S ANGRY DECEPTION
CONFUSED ABUSED LOST IN AGGRESSION
LOSING THE ABILITY OF HAVING REACTIONS
FROM THESE CRAZY SIGNS FALSIFIED PASSIONS
LIVING IN THIS WORLD WHO TO TRUST
LOST AND STAGNATED BLINDED THROUGH LUST
CRUEL INTENTIONS FULL OF EXPRESSION
ONLY THOROUGH MINDS WILL CAPTURE THIS LESSON
TREMBLING ENDEAVORS LOST IN DISCRETION
FLASHING LIGHTS SIMPLISTIC FASHION
NEGATIVE MINUS NEGATIVE THE SQUARE ROOT OF ZERO
ILL GOTTEN FRUITS FROM THIS UNKNOWN HERO
WALKING IN A TIME OF HOPELESS DEPRAVATION
FEELING ABUSE FROM THIS LONESOME SEPARATION
STUCK IN A REALM OF HARDSHIPS AND FRUSTRATION
ANGRY AGGRESSION FORCED INTO TEMPTATION
EMPTY PARADIGMS OF AN OBSOLETE HOST
RUNNING IN CIRCLES ON A BRAINSTORMING COAST
DRIFTING IN THE EMPTINESS OF THEATRICAL REBUTTALS
NOTHING TO SAY, SURROUNDED BY THESE TROUBLES
OF A WORD CRAZED INDIVIDUAL WHOSE MIND CRAVES
WAR
TRIPPING ON LIFE, KNOCKING ON HELL'S DOOR
TAMPERING WITH LIFE DEATH IS ON THE WAY
HIS EMPTY HEART HAS HIM STRESSED EVERYDAY
HE THROWS HIS TANTRUM BECAUSE OF THIS UNSOLVED
CULT
HE'S MAD AT GOD SO DEATH ISN'T HIS FAULT
HE THOUGHT ABOUT IT FOR A SECOND AND SAID THIS CAN'T
BE FAIR

HE REMEMBERED HE IS THE SON OF GOD HIS FATHER
CONTROLS THE AIR
HE TOOK A STEP BACK AND HE WIPED HIS EYES
HE REALIZED HE WAS ONLY FACING THESE TROUBLES
BECAUSE HE HIMSELF WAS A DISGUISE THIS SUDDEN
EPIPHANY CAUSED HIS NEW LIFE TO UNFOLD
GROWING INSTEAD OF GOING TURNED HIS BLACK COALS TO
GOLD

MENTORSHIP HELPS
BUILD YOUR SUCCESS!

Definition:

There is a saying that it takes a village to raise a child. I believe that to be true! No one got to where they are without some type of guidance that edged them along the way. Pay homage and continue to grow.

My reflection:

The Lincoln University of Pennsylvania changed my perception of life! I met many mentors at this prestigious institution that helped me build my character. Prior to Lincoln University, I have to give credit to my juvenile counselor Gary Priest. He was my first role model. He opened my eyes to the fact that doing what I thought was normal, which was acting like everyone else, was a weakness. I was 17 when I met Priest. He expressed to me that he would not let me be average, and he was not going to let me cop-out to be a "knucklehead," in his words.

Growing up in the hood, I didn't have a father figure to look up to, so when it came to Mr. Priest, I was abrasive. "This guy didn't care for me," I thought. I was so broken that I didn't trust anyone. I was too hurt; my mind frame was love gets you killed. All through my mishaps, he never gave up on me, and I will forever be grateful to him. Actually, he drove me up to Lincoln University with my one bag of clothes and said, "Son, this is where you become a man!" and "Don't you screw up because I'm gonna kick your ass!"

From the time I stepped foot on Lincoln soil, I began to develop as the leader I was born to be! All of my flaws and challenges I overcame. I give thanks to LU for bringing out the best of me. Ms. Sissy and Mr. Jerry for being so warm and welcoming to me. You see, the real reason why they mean so much to me is because I lost my grandmother, Louise Williams, when I was 11 years old. She was so near and dear to my heart, I was in the hospital when she passed. I couldn't express that hurt in words, which caused me to become defiant to everyone and led me down a path that I regret having gone down. When I met Ms. Sissy and Mr. Jerry, they filled a void and an emptiness in my life.

I also am sincerely appreciative of the Athletic Department at LU, especially Coach Jones and Coach Garfield- words cannot express the gratitude I owe these two guys. They literally took a chance on me. At that time, I was a felon locked up in prison and they didn't know me from a can of paint. They came to court and spoke on my behalf to the judge to allow me to come to LU. Even my first haircut while I was locked up came from Garfield. Coach Brian (Captain B) and Coach Gene taught me how to be a dog on the court and, more importantly, helped me be a great student athlete. They were in my corner the entire time through Lincoln University.

A professor of mine, Dr. Roberts, opened my mind about Black Awareness. It wasn't about the class he was teaching; he was about building **THE BLACK MAN**. Dr. Swinton learned of my background and embraced me as if I was his family. Stacey Tarlton gave me the courage to present professional Powerpoint presentations and didn't let me quit- my first professional conference was NASPA. Dean Ross' tough love strategies gave me the will to not accept or be anything other than great. Chief Woods, Capt. Conner, and Capt. Ruth strengthened my communication skills and developed me as a liaison from the students to the Admin.

I am also thankful for the Psychology Department, Dr. Favor, Dr. Gaither Hardy, and Dr. Kinsey for taking my raw knowledge and birthing me into the psychology world. They saw a diamond in the rough and polished it, it turned out to be me. I love them so much for never giving up on me. Omega Psi Phi Bloody Beta chapter taught me "Humility with Dignity, Humbleness with Pride." These brothers showed me what agape love is! Genyne L. Royal is the true definition of Leadership, she exemplifies everything that is positive and taught me weakness is never an option. I really don't know where to start with her because she is my heart. It's really hard to explain what she means to me. There are no comparisons when I think of her.

Dr. Bynum and Dr. Briggs, they are my true male role models! They accepted my flaws, adopted me as their own, and gave me hope when I didn't have any. Opening my eyes to a world I didn't even know existed, they changed my life completely. The Lincoln University of Pa.- "The first HBCU!"- tested all my weaknesses and helped build me into the man I am today.

There are more that were not mentioned but are equally important. I am writing this page to give hope to the youth who may have second thoughts about HBCU's. It's more than the education; it's the family setting, it's the student population, it's the forever friendships, it's the experience, it's the embracements. It's about mentorship. Trust me when I tell you, by far, one of the best decisions I made in my life was to attend an HBCU. From the bottom of my heart, thank you! From the words of my fellow Alumni Erica Campbell C/O 06, "1 8 5 4 first HBCU for Sure!"

Your reflection:

Take this time to jot down a few things that you are keeping with you along your journey from what you learned from your mentors.

_____

_____

_____

Who are your influences?

_____

_____

_____

What impact do they have on your life?

_____

_____

_____

Note:

There are positive and negative influences, figure out where you want to go in life, and seek a mentor that will guide you to the promised land. Great minds think alike, so the search will be easy! You got this! You are now ready to be an amazing leader!

POEM:

FREEEDOM!!!
LIVING, WORKING, PENS ARE CHIRPING RHYMES ARE
PERKING, MELODY IS AT ITS PEAK, LISTENING TO THE BEAT
WHILE TAPPING MY FEET I
GUESS
IT'S
FREEEDOM!!!!
RAISING POINTS UPON MY REQUEST
CHOOSING THE THINGS I WANT
NEVER FEEL STRESS!
I
GUESS
IT'S
FREEEDOM!!!
LIVING LIFE,
WALKING ACROSS THE BRIDGE OF OPPORTUNITY FIGHTING
FOR A THING CALLED UNITY
BLESSED TO BE IN THE COMMUNITY
I
Guess
IT'S
FREEEDOM!!!
BUT DON'T BE DUMB TO THIS WORLD
IT'S EASY TO SUCCUMB TO THIS EVIL THING THAT CAN BE
DISGUISED AS WISDOM
TO UNDERSTAND, YOU MUST REALLY READ BECAUSE THE
WEAPONS I WRITE
ARE PURPOSEFULLY MEANT TO FOLLOW THE CREED WHICH
MEANS
WE
NEED
FREEEDOM!!!

DON'T BE DEPRIVED, TOGETHER WE SHALL RISE BLACK ON
BLACK ALLIES, EYES TO THE SKY ON GOD WE WILL RELY
BECAUSE--
WE ARE FIGHTING FOR THE THING
WE
CALL
FREEEDOM!!!
WHO IS YALL?
REALIZING WE ARE FREE,
TOGETHERNESS—CALL US: "WE"
BELIEVING
THAT THERE COULD POSSIBLY BE A DAY THAT
WE
CALL
FREEE!!!
AND THAT MEANS
WE
WILL
HAVE
FREEEDOM!!
I BELIEVE I COULD SEE
A VISION FOR "WE"
US UPLIFTING EACH OTHER,
REALIZING WE ARE FREEE!!!
REALIZING WE ARE FREEE!!!
REALIZING
WE
ARE
FREEE!!!
BEHOLD THIS IS ME
WITH
A
NEED
FOR

69

FREEEDOM!!!
I AM MY OWN BOSS
I WILL FIGHT FOR ALL IT COSTS
BECAUSE I REFUSE TO BE LOST
IN A WORLD WITH
NO
GOT
DAMN
FREEEDOM!!!!
TRIALS AND TRIBULATIONS
SUCCESS IS THE REVELATION
FOCUSING ON THAT GREAT STAR **"ASPIRATION"** STANDING
TALL
I
YELL
FREEEDOM!!!

AFTERWARD

I want to thank you for allowing me to share different parts of my life's experiences . I hope you enjoyed the ride. I gave you some jewels of how to jumpstart or further your cause in life. I am truly thrilled that you are going to become the best you that you can possibly be! I speak prosperity in your life, I believe that you will apply what you learned in your life and you will become a success story versus a statistic. Mediocre no longer has a spot in your life. You are destined to be amongst the elite, you have a story to tell and I believe in you. You can accomplish your dreams, you will muster up the faith, you will believe in yourself enough to help you jump over any hurdle that gets in the way of your path to success. I know that once you manifest your inner beast that there will be nothing that stops you. I speak great energy and focus in your life. There will be no hindrances that will stop your greatness. You are on this earth to make a difference in someone's life. You are special, you are a unique individual, no one was made the same. I believe you will find your inner *Chi*/balance/powerful energy/Inner guardian angel. All I charge you with is once you better yourself don't keep it to yourself! <u>LIFE</u> is about **Service, Uplifting, Unselfishness,** and becoming a **Beacon of your community.**

Because you are so awesome and made it thus far, I have composed a bonus section compiled of short poems that will surely keep you entertained. I am horrible with disclaimers when it comes to expressionist pieces. So strap up and enjoy! Thank you again, for allowing me to share my life.

PART 2

LIGHT POEMS

I AM GROWN

I AM A WRITER STRAPPED UP WITH AMMUNITION,
POETIC, ENERGETIC, WITH A SHORT CLIP OF AMBITION
MY STYLE IS DRIVEN WITH A PASSION FOR LIVING
THE IMAGE IS SO VIVID FROM THE WORDS I'M GIVING

I AM GROWN

THE IMAGES ARE SURREAL FROM THE WORDS YOU FEEL
A GRATEFUL PURPOSE,HEAVENLY ORDEAL
UNLOCK THE DOOR, BELIEVE IT, IT'S REAL
MY FOOD IS TRUTH! HONESTY IS MY SPILL

I AM GROWN

REFRESH
I'M UPLOADING MY FAITH, I'M LIVING MY LIFE
I'M ESCAPING THE HATE
MY FRIEND

I AM GROWN

I'M LIVING MY WILL EXPRESSION IS THE DEAL
UNDERSTAND TO HEAL UNDERSTOOD I'M REAL REFRESH
I FEEL THE LIFE I'M LIVING NO STRIFE
I WANT TO STARE AT THE GLARE OF MY FUTURE WIFE

I AM GROWN

A Gift From Woo!

MY HEART SCREAMS FOR SOMETHING!
WHAT COULD IT BE?
A LOUD ROARING SOUND
IS SCREAMING AT ME.
SO IT YELLS AND YELLS
IT'S SCREENING MY SOUL!
I'M WONDERING IS IT ME?
OR
IS IT A LIE THAT'S BEING TOLD?
I TAKE MY TIME AND I LISTEN TO MY THOUGHTS BUT MY
HEART IS ON FIRE!
SCREAMING!
HEY!
AM I LISTENING TO YOUR SYMPATHETIC THOUGHTS? I
START SMILING
BECAUSE MY HEART WAS TRYING TO PLAY ME, SO I SAID
"YOU GOT IT"!
THEN THE NEXT WORDS WERE
'YOUNGIN' GET AWAY FROM ME!
SO I STOPPED,
AND AS I WAS GETTING READY TO WALK AWAY I HEARD
WAIT!
IS IT LOVE THAT I SMELL COMING FROM YOUR WAY? I SAID
"NO!"
"NO!"
"YOU WON'T GET ME LIKE THAT THIS TIME". AS I PAUSED,
THIS DIVINE INTERVENTION RELUCTANTLY TOOK OVER MY
MIND,
AND MY THOUGHTS WERE PARALYZED,
I THEN REALIZED
MAYBE THAT THIS DISEASE
OVER SHADOWING ME?

THE DISEASE IS THIS LOVE THING
THAT FLEW ITS WAY AT ME;
BY A SNEEZE,
HU-CHEW,
"BLESS YOU!"
EVER SINCE I LAID MY EYES ON YOU,
HU-CHEW!
I REALIZE THAT
THE BLESSING WAS YOU,
HU-CHEW,
IS IT YOU!
THAT TURNED ME FROM BEING BLUE!
IT MUST BE YOU
BECAUSE IT WAS THE SNEEZE
THAT GAVE ME THE FLU!
WHICH MEANS
BABY O BABY
I
LOVE
YOU!

MUSIC LOVE

WE LOVE THAT GOOD OLE FUNK
MUSIC BLASTING ALL CLASSICS NO JUNK
A HUNDRED SONGS TO LAST THROUGH THE WHOLE NIGHT A
GROOVY PLAYLIST, SO BLISS! THERE IS NO ROOM TO FIGHT
LISTENING TO THE BEACH SOUNDS OF THE MUSICAL TREND
ENOUGH TO LAY BACK, AND SIP HENNY TIL THE BOTTLES
END DAYS OF WONDER, SO PEACEFUL TO STARE
LIVING IN BLUNDER WITH THIS TRANQUIL AIR
MELODY IS THE SOUND, OUR BLISS HAS REACHED ITS PEAK
WONDERING, SITTING, LISTENING, NOT AN ECHO TO LEAK
THE TUNE IS WHISPERING, I'M WATCHING YOU AS YOUR
SOUL STARES. KISSING YOUR SOFT LIPS, ENJOYING YOUR
WARM AIR. I'M HERE WITH YOU, YOU ARE HERE WITH YOUR
FRIEND NIGHTS LIKE THIS I WISH; IT WOULD NEVER END
CANDLES ARE LIT, WITH SWEET SMELLS OF TEA
OUR BODIES ARE CONNECTED. TOGETHER LIKE IT'S MEANT
TO BE.
WE STILL ARE IN THIS ROOM SO QUIET, SO MUCH PEACE
LOVING THIS MOMENT AS WE BEGIN TO RELEASE
WE'RE STEADY HOLDING EACH OTHER IN THE MIDDLE OF
THIS ROOM REALIZING WE STARTED OUR OWN MUSIC
FROM THIS AUTUMN'S BLOOM WELL
WE ALL KNOW ALL GOOD THINGS COME TO AN END
A WHISPER I HEARD COMING FROM MY MUSIC HATING ASS
FRIEND IT'S TIME TO GO GIRL!!!
DAMN

SWEET SLUMBER......

GIVINGFUL MOMENT LONG LASTING PEACE
LIVING IN THE STRESS- LESS TIME, THE FEELINGS HAS
INCREASED PLAYING IN YOUR WATERS UNTIL YOUR
STREAMS DISPERSE
I FELL IN TOO DEEP! FOR NOT TESTING THE WATERS FIRST
I VENTURED THROUGH THE WHOLE MOUNTAIN JUST TO GET
TO YOUR STREAM YOUR WATER RUNS DEEP, I'M IN A POOL
FULL OF DREAMS
I SWAM THROUGH THE POOL JUST TO REALIZE I WAS THE
FISH OF YOUR SWEET AROMA SMELLS THAT GRANTED ME A
WISH MY WISH CAME TRUE, SLIDING IN THIS PRECIOUS
DOVE
WHO WOULDN'T WANT TO BE SWIMMING IN THIS POOL
FULL OF LOVE WATERS SO FRESH JUST TO MAKE ME TASTE
DRINK IT TO THE LAST DROP NOT A DRIP TO WASTE
LONG STROKE, BACKSTROKE, I AM SWIMMING IN YOUR
STREAM BELIEVE ME WHEN I TELL YOU; I AM LOVING YOUR
CREAM
YOUR WAVES ARE RUMBLING I BECAME ONE WITH YOUR
HIPS YOU CLENCHED YOUR RELEASE MY MIND STARTED
DOING FLIPS I FLOATED IN YOUR PUDDLES JUST AS
MARVELOUS AS IT SEEMS ONLY TO WAKE UP AND FIND
OUT! IT WAS ALL A WET DREAM.............

-

MS YOU GOT ME LIKE WOWWW

IM CHECKING FOR YOU
HELLO SWEETS I PEEPED YOUR STYLE
I AM GLAZING IN YOUR EYES I'M INTRIGUED BY YOUR SMILE
MS YOU GOT ME LIKE WOWWW
IM DIGGING THE WAY YOU TALK
YOU HAVE THIS UMPH BEHIND YOUR WALK
MS YOU GOT ME LIKE WOWWW
I BEEN WATCHING HOW YOU MOVE THE CROWD
I SEE FIRST HAND HOW YOU MAKE A GROWN MAN
FEEL LIKE A CHILD
MS YOU GOT ME LIKE WOWWW
WHEN I SEE YOU I GET NERVOUS I GET MIXED IN MY WORDS
IT'S LIKE WHEN I'M LOOKING AT YOU MY NOUNS TURNS
INTO MY VERBS
AND JESUS OH JESUS DID I MENTION YOUR PRECIOUS
CURVES
MS YOU GOT ME LIKE WOWWW
I LOVE YOUR NATURAL HAIR, I LOVE THE FACT YOU FEEL
COMFORTABLE IN YOUR OWN SKIN NOWADAYS THAT'S
RARE AND I KNOW ME PLUS YOU EQUALS A WIN
I APOLOGIZE BUT
MS YOU GOT ME LIKE WOWWW
I'
I'M FEELING LIKE THE FEELING IS MUTUAL I CAN HEAR IT IN
YOUR VOICE
IM WATCHING YOU AND YOU'RE WATCHING ME, WE ARE
STUDYING EACH OTHER'S POISE
MS YOU GOT ME LIKE WOWWW
THIS IS THE BEGINNING, OF THIS LOVE BIRD STORY,
WHEN LOVE FINDS EACH OTHER TO GOD GETS THE GLORY!
MS YOU GOT ME LIKE WOWWW
THE END

A Princess Turned Queen

YOU ALWAYS GAVE ME HOPE WHEN PEOPLE TOLD ME I WAS
WRONG
YOU ARE THE REASONS FOR MY SUCCESS YOU'RE THE
REASON I CAME ALONG. NEVER FEEL DISCOURAGED WITH
ANYTHING YOU DO
CAUSE THERE IS ALWAYS A "ME" TO LOVE A "YOU" TO BE
TRUE.
IT'S HARD TO EXPLAIN THE CREDIT I OWE
CAUSE YOU MADE IT SO EASY FOR MY GIFT TO FLOW
I DON'T THINK YOU UNDERSTAND THE WORDS THAT YOU
GAVE ME WHEN I DIDN'T HAVE THEM FOR MYSELF
YOU WERE MY ENERGY YOU REVIVED MY HEALTH
IT'S BEEN 30 YEARS THAT'S ALL MY LIFE
YOU'VE ALWAYS BEEN SOMETHING SPECIAL AND TRUE
CHARACTERISTICS OF A WIFE
WHEN EVERYONE DISOWNED ME YOUR WORDS HELPED ME
REFORM
YOUR EYES MADE ME SETTLE, YOUR HEART CALMED MY
STORM
I'VE BEEN TO JUVEYS, JAIL, AND PRISON; SOME OF THE
TOUGHEST PLACES THAT PEOPLE CAN BE YOU ARE THE ONLY
ONE IN THE WORLD THAT CAN MAKE ME MUSHY IN THE
PRESENT OF THE QUEEN MS ROYALTY
SO WHEN IT'S ALL SAID AND DONE I WANT YOU TO PRINT
THIS AND POST THIS ON YOUR WALL
FOR ALL YOUR HATERS THAT'S DYING TO SEE YOU FALL
JUST KNOW YOU HAVE THE TITLE OF THE "BEST OF THE
BESTIES" FRIENDS TO THE END YOU ARE MY MOTIVATOR
THE WIND THAT PUSHES MY PEN

DRIFT

LATE NIGHT DRIFT WATCHING YOU AS IT RAINS
THE STATE OF MY MIND IS SPAWNED THROUGH THESE
PAINS
TREMBLING TARNISH ADDRESSING IS STRANGE
NOT ONE HAS UNDERSTOOD THAT THIS MESSAGE IS FAR
RANGE
RUMBLE IN THE JUNGLE ANIMAL ON THE BRAIN
HOW CAN ONE LIVE AND ALSO MAINTAIN
A SCORPION STING VERSES A SUB ZERO REIGN
WHO DARE TO BE SIMPLE? NONE OF THIS IS PLAIN
DRIFTING FOR THE MOMENT STUCK WITH NO PEACE
ONE LIFE TO LIVE ADDED STRUGGLE IS IN HIS LEASE
MENTIONED IN THE STORIES HOW HE RAGES THROUGH THE
STREET FACED WITH GLORY... TURMOIL TURNS TO HEAT
UNDERMINED PUPPET STUCK IN BAD WAYS
TRIPPING OFF LIFE PRAYING FOR BETTER DAYS
NOT ONE IS RIGHT IN THE TRIPLE NUMBER STAGE
DO THY WILL IS THE EMBLEM OF RAGE
NO ONE KNOWS! HAS THE TRUTH TAKEN FLIGHT?
OR IS IT THE GHOULS THAT CAUSED THIS HUMANISTIC
FRIGHT?
WATCHING THE WORLD FOLKS FULL OF FEAR
MUMBLING AND BUMBLING BEWARE OF THE SCARE
EVERYONE IS WATCHING DESPERATION IS HERE
INTRUSIVE UNDERMINING GOALS CAN BE COMPLACENT
THROUGH THERE WALKING THROUGH THE NIGHT NO
SANITY ON THE SCENE
SEEING IS BELIEVING AND THERE'S NO SUNSHINE FOR THE
UNKEEN NO ONE KNOWS OF THIS MORTIFIED SCHEME
GET YOUR LIFE TOGETHER FOR YOU ARE IN A MIXED UP
DREAM

TRUE DIVINE

TRUE DIVINE I LOVE MY FRAT,
YOU WISH YOU COULD KNOW BUT YOU CAN'T HANDLE
THAT
TOO MUCH INFO WITH A GANG OF ORDEALS
I WOULD LET YOU KNOW BUT YOU AIN'T ON THE REAL
MARCHING, AND GROOVING! HOPING IN THE SHOW
WE ARE THE BEST AND WHOLE THE WORLD KNOWS
STOMPING ON FRATS WE BE BREAKING THE RULES
WE DO OUR BEST TO RUN OUR SCHOOLS
THE GIFT AND THE CURSE! BRANDED OR TATTED SOLDIER
ONLY GOOD BRUHS
KNOW WHY MY CUP RUNNETH OVER
I HAD A GREAT LIFE WITH OMEGA IT'S BETTER
I WENT THROUGH BLOOD, SWEAT, AND TEARS TO WRITE
THIS LETTER I'M NEVER ALONE I WILL ALWAYS HAVE
FRIENDS
21 QUESTIONS MY BOND NEVER ENDS
I DON'T KNOW ABOUT YOUR FRAT BUT, I WILL ALWAYS
LOVE MINE TO DEATH DO US APART! THANK GOD TO BE
APART OF THE NINE

DARK POEMS

REAL LIFE

A CELEBRATION OF LIFE OR A LONG LASTING CURSE
WHO CARES?? LISTEN UP WHILE I FINISH MY VERSE
GOOD OR BAD LOVE OR HATE
WHO DARES TO STAND CHASING THIS FATE
HONORABLE FASHION OR FORGETFUL KILL
ARE YOU PREPARED FOR THE CHAMBERLAINS WILL
DISCREET OR WIDE OPEN
CRAZY LIVES DESIRES HOPING
THAT ONE-DAY YOU SEE TURMOIL DEFEAT
KEEP LISTENING YOU WILL CATCH THIS BEAT
RUSH THIS RUSH EYES OVERSEE
ONE EYE ON YOU 8 EYES ON ME
THE CREEPER LIES OF DECEPTION
ILL LOATHSOME FEELINGS OF TROUBLESOME PROTECTION
THE LESSON IS ALMOST THE TERM
ONLY IF U KNEW THIS AFFECTIONST GERM
MISSIONS LOVE FILTHY PAST
ARE U PREPARED TO HANDLE THE WRATH

Believe Me

CHARISMATIC THOUGHTS EVERYBODY LOVES WISHING
HOPING AND PRAYING THAT THEY SEE BLESSINGS IN THE
MISSION REALIZING THEY CAN'T LOSE FROM THE UNSUNG
AMBITION
BUT UNTOLD STORIES HAVE YOU LOST IN COMPETITION
REALIZING THE TRUTH; THAT WAS SAID WAS
CONTRADICTING
WRESTLING WITH FAITH ANALYZING YOUR LIVING
NOW YOU LOST IN A WORLD WHERE THAT LIE IS THE
PROVISION
EMPTINESS THOUGHTS HAVE YOU MAKING THE WRONG
DECISION WONDERING IS THERE ANY HOPE OUT HERE IN
THIS DOMINION?
MY MIND IS POURING, MY HEART IS SOARING,
I'M LOSING CONTROL, I'M NOT YELLING I'M ROARING,
I GO BEYOND BELIEF MY HEART RATES BEATS,
LOST IN THE TROUBLE, CRAZY AND DECEIT,
STUCK IN THE PUDDLES, NO TIME FOR TREATS.
I BELIEVE IN KARMA SO THIS MIGHT BE THE BEAST,
TRAPPED IN THE WORLD ALL I SEE IS THE STREET.
I'M LOSING CONTROL, I'M WALKING THE BEAT,
WHO ARE YOU? WHO IS ME?
WHAT YOU DON'T GET, YOU WILL NEVER SEE.
DON'T ASK JUST BELIEVE ME!!!!!!!

IT'S OVER……

I GUESS OVER TIME THINGS GROW APART.
HOWEVER, IF YOU HAVE THE LOVE, THINGS MIGHT GO BACK
TO THE START. A LOT OF THINGS DON'T CHANGE EXCEPT
WHEN IT'S DEALING WITH THE HEART. IT'S LIKE YOU THINK
YOU FOUND LOVE BUT SOMETHING JUST CRASHES AT YOUR
HEART!
IT'S UNEXPLAINABLE BECAUSE YOU THINK YOU HAVE
MUTUAL THOUGHTS, BUT ONCE YOU SEE PAST ENDEAVORS,
IT KIND OF RUINS YOUR THOUGHTS. YOU SEE THIS THING
FROM THE CLOSEST POINT OF VIEW, AND STILL CAN'T
GRASP A WHOLE OF IT BECAUSE YOU WERE BLIND FROM
THE BEGINNING.
BUT ONCE YOU FOUND IT NO MATTER WHAT NO ONE
WANTS AN ENDING. THE FEELING SORRIES IS HERE, PLUS
MISERY AND DEFEAT.
YOU CAN'T LET YOURSELF CHANGE; FEELING AT THE
BOTTOM UNDER THE FEET. THIS MEANS LOST TREASURE
ALMOST FORGOTTEN,
FRUITS YOU LOVE SPOILED ROTTEN,
TRYING TO FIND THAT LOVE AGAIN BUT PRIDE HAS BEEN
MOCKING.
IT'S CRAZY TO THINK HOW PRIDE CAN PAINT YOUR PICTURE.
THE MOOD WAS RIGHT UNTIL YOU LET THAT CRAZY GLITCH
ENTER.
NOW THAT IT'S OVER I GUESS IT'S TIME TO MOVE ON.
ALL THE LOVE THAT WAS THERE, FOR THAT FRUIT HAS
BECOME FOREIGN. I GUESS OVER TIME, THINGS GROW
APART,
WITHOUT THE LOVE TO HOLD THINGS TOGETHER THERE IS
NO NEED TO GO BACK TO THE START. IT'S OVER……

REST IN HEAVEN

I KNOW I HAVE TO BE STRONG BECAUSE YOU ARE ALWAYS
WITH ME
YOUR BODY HAS LEFT THIS WORLD AND YOUR SPIRIT IS
NOW FREE
YOU BLESSED US WITH YOUR CHARM YOUR LOVE YOUR
PASSION DEEP INSIDE YOU MY BROTHER MY BESTFRIEND
MY DAWG I CAN ALWAYS GO TO CONFIDE IT'S HARD FOR
ME TO MAKE THIS POEM BECAUSE I NEVER THOUGHT IT
WOULD BE THAT YOU AND I WOULD BE WRITING ABOUT
BUT I KNOW NOW YOU ARE FINALLY FREE FROM THE PAIN
THIS CRUDDY WORLD HAD FOR YOU
YOUR BODY HAS BEEN FREED, YOUR SPIRIT HAS BEEN TOO
I CAN HEAR YOUR WORDS CLEARLY TELLING ME TO BE
TOUGH
BUT YOU KNOW MY HEART AND BRO IT'S GOING TO BE
ROUGH
BUT FOR YOU I HAVE TO BE STRONG THERE'S NO OTHER
WAY
YOUR SPIRIT IS IN HEAVEN WATCHING ME EVERYDAY
I WAS WITH YOU WHEN YOU PRAYED, YOU HAVE
ACCOMPLISHED THAT GOAL TO BE WITH JESUS IN HEAVEN,
GOD SAVED YOUR SOUL
REST IN HEAVEN BRO! I LOVE YOU

ACKNOWLEDGEMENTS

I WANT TO GIVE THANKS TO GOD FIRST, MY FAMILY, SISTERS, BROTHERS, NIECES, NEPHEWS, AUNTS, AND UNCLES, FOR THEIR SUPPORT. MAXINE AUDIAN, ANDRE GILLUM (RIP). LINCOLN UNIVERSITY, AND CENTRAL STATE UNIVERSITY FOR ALLOWING ME TO FURTHER MY EDUCATION. THE BODYGUARD AND ENTERTAINMENT INDUSTRY FOR ALL THAT TRUSTED ME WITH THEIR LIFE, AND MY BODYGUARD BROTHERS THAT WAS HOLDING IT DOWN WITH ME, WE DON'T GET THAT MUCH CREDIT! ALL MY COWORKERS I EVER WORKED WITH, I RESPECT AND THANK YOU. MY FRIENDS AND EVERYONE THAT I EVER MET, EVEN IF IT WAS ONE ENCOUNTER. BALTIMORE FOR SHAPING MY MORALS AND PRINCIPLES. COACH RIVERS, AND POPS, THERE WOULDN'T BE A LINCOLN UNIVERSITY WITHOUT THE SUPPORT OF THEM. AS WELL AS THOSE THAT STOOD BY MY SIDE WHEN I NEEDED YA'LL THE MOST. MY GUYS 2100, 1500, NEVER FORGET WHERE I COME FROM. UNCLE RAY WIZARD FOR EMBRACING ME AND BECOMING MY FAMILY. SHOUTS OUT TO MY BEST FRIENDS, AND THE CIRCLE. ALSO IF I MISSED YOU, YOU ARE EQUALLY IMPORTANT IN MY LIFE.

SPECIAL THANKS TO THE HONORABLE JUDGE ALFRED NANCE FOR GIVING ME AN OPPORTUNITY TO CHANGE MY LIFE!

Made in the USA
Middletown, DE
16 May 2022

65817804R00056